Breathing Under Water

Breathing Under Water

Poems by
Paulette Roeske

*For Jason —
one poetry lover
to another —
Paulette*

Stormline Press
Urbana Illinois
1988

*College of Lake County
February 13, 1991*

Copyright © 1988 by Paulette Roeske

All rights reserved. Except for the purpose of a brief review, no part of this book may be reproduced in any form without permission in writing from the publisher.

International Standard Book Number: 0-935153-08-X

Stormline Press, Inc.
P.O. Box 593
Urbana Illinois 61801

Manufactured in the United States of America

Publication of this book is made possible in part by a grant from the Illinois Arts Council, a state agency.

Acknowledgment is made to the editors of the following publications in which some of these poems first appeared:

American Poetry Anthology: "Report from Marina Towers"
Another Chicago Magazine: "A Gift Twice-Given," "The Sickness of the Body"
Anthology of Magazine Verse & Yearbook of American Poetry: "7:00 A.M. Lakefront," reprinted from *Poetry*
Ascent: "The Bus Driver Dreams of Blue Island," "How the Twentieth Century Betrayed the Last Christian Martyr," "Mother, Retelling the News"
B-City: "Dream at Easter"
Chicago Review: "Venus de Milo: Her Final Complaint"
Cottonwood Review: "Salmon, After Magritte"
The Denny Poems 1985-1986 (anthology): "Strasbourg in the Spring: A Guided Walk"
Hawaii Review: "Island"
Indiana Review: "Lost," "Waiting for This"
Kansas Quarterly: "Again"
New Laurel Review: "Questions"
Overtures: "Two Mallards," "Two Women"
Poetry: "Looking for You One Year Later," "Refugees at Avila Beach," "7:00 A.M. Lakefront," "Wintering at a Summer Resort"
Tendril: "A Plan to Circumvent the Death of Beauty"
The Virginia Quarterly Review: "Aquarium," "Under Glass"
Webster Review: "Edens Expressway: An Ode," "Anger"
Whetstone: "Report from Marina Towers," reprinted from *American Poetry Anthology*
Woman Poet: The Midwest (anthology): "A Little Drama," "Going Under," "Snake in the Yard"
"Waiting for This" was also printed as a broadside by Illinois Writers, Inc.

My thanks to College of Lake County for granting me the time to complete this book.

My thanks also to Sara Fieberg, Janet Segal, and to my teacher Lisel Mueller for her kindness and encouragement.

for Addie

CONTENTS

I

Wintering at a Summer Resort 11
Island 12
Two Women 13
Snake in the Yard 14
A Gift Twice-Given 15
Talking to My Sister 16
Salmon, After Magritte 18
Driving into Rain 19
A Little Drama 20
Report from Marina Towers 21
The Bus Driver Dreams of Blue Island 22
Getting There 24
My Father's House, First Snow 25
Again 26

II

Lost 29
The Pyromaniac and the Heat Wave 31
Mother, Retelling the News 32
My Student, Talking 33
Under Glass 34
Questions 35
Liar 36
Waiting for This 37
Dream at Easter 39
Aquarium 40
Anger 42

What She Knows   43

The Sickness of the Body   44

Dreaming of the Dead   45

Bending to Look Through Your Eyes   47

A Plan to Circumvent the Death of Beauty   48

Going Under   49

III

Refugees at Avila Beach   53

Regarding Marie Antoinette   54

Edens Expressway: An Ode   55

Shortcut Through the Park   56

Venus de Milo: Her Final Complaint   57

Dreamer, 3:00 A.M.   59

Two Mallards   60

Tropics   61

Ground Blizzard   62

How the Twentieth Century Betrayed the Last Christian Martyr   63

Looking for You One Year Later   65

Harbor Seal   66

7:00 A.M. Lakefront   67

Strasbourg in the Spring: A Guided Walk   68

Waking in Another Country   69

Riding the Back Bay Trail   71

Jade Cove   73

I

Wintering at a Summer Resort

Horses drop their heads against the cold
and paw the battered grass. A heifer
in the next pasture cranes her stubborn neck,
strips bark from a willow.
Past the fields, a two room cottage
where a hanger-on put laundry on the line.
Too stiff to flap.

The wood is without
the confusion of foliage.
Hunters stand idle,
sighting down long barrels at flying clouds.
A peeling sign creaks BUD & RAMONA'S,
BUD & RAMONA'S, but Bud and Ramona are busy
in the back room.

The lake is the color of nothing-to-do.
A black snake tracks a frog,
snaps at the fleshy belly.
Bud and Ramona, friendly under their quilt,
are not concerned. There is always time,
no boats in the harbor, summer debris
awash on the freezing shore.

Island

A reef encircles it, separating
the sea from reasonable waves
near land. Here, they say,
no shark can break through, but
in California a newspaper photograph
shows only the wetsuit, laid out like a corpse,
right side gaping. The family
lives with absence.

When we dive, I want my daughter
to admire the fluted coral, to think of it
as an arm around her waist. We drop
over the edge. Quiet fins, cilia waving.
Hello.

We sprawl on the surface
like uprooted ferns. Breath
returns through the snorkel
like a patient's, safe in his hospital tent.

The water erupts beside me.
She jerks upright, her mask off,
sputtering salt from her nose and mouth.
She tries to run, contradicting
the waves' logic.

Out of the water, I see her ankles
bleeding from the coral's explicit touch.
She holds herself, rocking like a small boat.

Two Women

The woman at the corner of Chicago and Main
knots her hair and counts the cars.
Her jaw hangs. Her words
slide out of control.
I suspect there is no reason to stare
in this city where women fall in the street,
where there is no visible threat but the sun
swelling like a red infection.

Only fifteen years ago, great-aunt Marie
counted eggs in her cellar. *Eins...Zwei...Drei...*
Her hair went from black to yellow,
the thin braids wound in a knot
held with wicket pins.
She slapped the fat hens from their nests
and took the warm brown eggs.
Fire spat in the kitchen
where the chicks were sick in their wire cage.
She dragged them one by one,
gripping their delicate legs with her square fingers,
and cracked their heads
against the open furnace door.
There is no reason to remember
how they burned, or the eager fire.

Snake in the Yard

It is probably innocent, traveling
across the stone path from rhubarb to squash
as best it can. I spring back
anyway. Father, with one thoughtless foot,
sends it flapping through the branches
of a stunted apricot.
Startled jays scatter, the snake
twists among them in the late sun.

I walk with quick steps back to the house.
Father stays behind
shading his eyes in the glare,
hoping to glimpse it
slipping uncrippled into the tall grass.

A Gift Twice-Given

I'm home where grey spawns grey,
where the rub of two perfect surfaces
exceeds sight, where the fishing gull wings them both.

It's quiet on a late fall afternoon
with threat of rain, but an old woman
buttoned into her coat hurries across
the sand. She wants to talk.
She tells me the dark spots back in the grass
are wild rose, an elegant idea.

She gives my daughter a lucky stone. Says
hold it up and watch the lake
through two aligned holes. The child looks,
then turns. "For you."

Talking to My Sister

Every day of this visit
the desert heat presses down
upon the town. At night
we escape the airless house
where our daughters sleep
and circle the block
in our waltz-length nightgowns,
heedless as girls.
We talk about our family,
all the women —
mothers, daughters, sisters,
and the men — dead,
divorced, absent as landlords.
The hot wind whips our gowns
so they stick to our legs and hips.

You say the low-lying hills
have always held the town
like capable arms,
but now the brittle grass
goads the fire up the slopes
transfixing us with fresh surprise
each time we turn the corner.

Sometimes our words, wayward
as ash, are lost
in the helicopters' sputter.
They hover above us,
full-bellied, water-heavy,
their cargo useless
in the rushing wind.

We keep our eyes on the flames,
as if our stares could stop
the leap from hill to hill
to roof or worse,
but still we keep talking
even while imagining
what we each would save.

Salmon, After Magritte

On this late night walk along the lake,
I find a coho half buried in sand.
Iris and pupil, pouting lips, each small tooth
is human. If I were daring,
would I discover unscaled legs
muscular from arguing their way
through the great lake?

I look closer for a sign. A raised fin,
an almost imperceptible lift of breast,
some hint of kinship. I have no proof.
Just the painter who warmed his palette
with one dab of sienna, enough
for half a woman.

Driving into Rain

The music on the Midwest radio sounds
African on this particular day
because each mile is darker than the last.

Anything could happen out here.
Verdant pines, ragged as lightning, stagger
across the horizon. Birds forget their formation
and dip crazily.

The music is more urgent now.
A blowing branch is the emerald flash
of a jungle parrot, the windshield wipers spastic.

I drive through some anonymous town
where rows of elms line the wet streets.
Men and women chatter in colorful groups
in front of a picture window.
They hold their wine glasses at careful angles.
The quiet moon of the porch light
illuminates a fern, spiny, safe.

A Little Drama

The wren house sways on its long pole
like another tree.
Father spits over his balcony. He's old.
He remembers the time a wren
died in the hole he cut too small
to admit its living body. It lodged
there limply, later swelling tight as a plug.
He climbed the ladder
hearing his heart in his ears.
It was that still.

He popped the body out with his stubby fingers
and tossed it in the slough
on limbs broken by the last storm.
The others know. Now they sit
on their shingled roof and rasp their little rage.
They fly somewhere else to sleep.

Report from Marina Towers

There are no boats on the river
today, but the water is just as deep
as yesterday when I stood at the bridge,
when one quick spring would have forced
the patient green to close over my head
and smooth into a smiling mouth.

At noon I study the carpet: an oriental archer
elegant on his horse, a leaping doe
his arrow cannot reach. They glide
around the room while the river at my back
unravels its pale green story, telling itself
to no one in particular.

The Bus Driver Dreams of Blue Island

The bus is empty
except for one beautiful woman
who missed her stop.
She doesn't know where she is
and by now she doesn't care.
When she comes to the front of the bus
and leans over me, her dark hair
falls around her face and keeps falling
until I can barely see the man at the corner
waving his arms. Because the light
is green, I step on the accelerator
and call, "Next stop Blue Island."

She laughs and settles into my lap.
We pass the Michigan Avenue stores
brimming with desire where the mannequins' eyes
droop like dead fish. Heading south,
she thinks the signs on the burnt out
buildings are swastikas
but I tell her this is still America.
I open the windows and we listen
to the boozy music. She takes
off her coat and dances. I give her
castanets from the map compartment.
We pass cities from which no light
escapes, and the wind moans
around the corners of stone buildings.

When the last street dead ends,
waves break around the launched bus
with a sound like urgent wings.
We tear the city maps into strips
and trail them from the windows.
She tells me she believes in Blue Island.
Then the circling herons veer so close
we hear their pumping hearts
and the mountains bloom from the sea,
their dark foliage encouraging us
to name them Blue Mountains.

I swing open the doors for the last time
and recognize this as home to all the lost
light, and because every gesture
is always necessary and right,
when I step down the sand admires my feet
and the beautiful woman accepts my proffered hand.
She waits for me to say,
"When I kiss you, you will not awake."

Getting There

Fagan's Park is under water.
We're forced to the wood
where shoots struggle,
where each inch of growth
is important.

You, my child,
scramble in the rubble
of a burnt out vacation cabin.
Moss clings to the foundation.
You take my hand tighter.
You want me to read
words scrawled on the wall in blue.
I lie to you. Tell you
they mean nothing

and dream past the ruin
to an interloper's dream:
repairing the fence,
replacing the glass,
raising the shade
on a bright morning

but only far enough
to see the first crocus
nursed by mulch,
the gate latched.

My Father's House, First Snow

The hills behind my father's house
invite these tireless tobogganers
the weather doesn't scare,
zig-zagging down the long run
between plum and apricot
(my father's trees)
their trunks whip-thin.
At the bottom, the track
plunges across the frozen creek
that took a life one summer.

And there is my father among children
by the grape arbor at the foot of the hill,
pulling the sled made by his father.
From where I watch through the window
of my father's house, he is young
in his aviator cap, flaps over his ears,
mufflered and bundled, his face
a tiny moon almost lost
on the white landscape.
I don't think he sees me seeing him
regret the steep hill
or my daughter who now expects
another easy ride. He pulls the rope
taut over this shoulder, his sigh
visible in the frozen air.
He starts up the hill again.

Again

The sea invites you in,
offering the promise of abandon
you have always wanted. You leave
your tedious clothes on the shore

and enter like a minor god. It is warm
and, as in a movie, colorful fish
dart around your legs. You begin

to swim away from yourself. As your strokes
grow more powerful, you smile and wave at passing fish
like royalty acknowledging the crowd.

*

On shore, your hesitant body
considers the water.
When a stingray cruises past
you look for the tail hook,
weapon against careless waders
who think earth is not enough.
But still you marvel at the frilled edges
of its foreign shape,
how it breathes under water.

Past the stingray, far out
past the protective reef, you see
the legs of your perfect self intersect the horizon
like flukes sounding another goodbye.

II

Lost

The woman in the green economy car
waits in stalled rush hour traffic.
Working the last shift, her day begins
at night. Stuck behind the blank
backside of a Federal Armored Express,
she imagines an aerial view, an open place
where cars move freely, unbounded by lanes or limits,
their efficient engines transported.
She imagines them whirring off like helicopters,
finally having made more of themselves.

This gap in attention sends her cloverleafing
to some other destination. She inadvertently follows
the Armored Express to a strange city where the streets
have deliberate names — Aptakisic, Narragansett, Coffin
Road, yes, she is telling the truth. Stopped at the tracks,
she can see the end of a long train, but it shuts down
in front of her, blocking the road, lights flashing.
Is this the third train or the same train
for the third time? A smug child on a bicycle
jerks up the handlebars and coasts past
on the back wheel. He knows his way home to the brick
bungalow where his family waits without worry.
His mother uses all four burners to prepare the dinner.

She has lost the Armored Express and looks for another
reason to keep driving. The cities dovetail
like so many cars on the freight. On the tape deck,
Ashkenazy plays a dirge. She eats an apple
and tosses the core into the back seat with the others.
Exiting to the next tollway, the traffic is fast paced.
She has found the unimaginable opening. A state cop
razzle-dazzles his way past her, six antennas waving
Move Over, three shining lanes his for the taking.
She does not know she will pass him up near the state line,
hubcap deep in meridian mire, wheels still spinning.
North may have been a mistake. It almost never ends.

She turns off on a country road,
believing she has reached the interior.
Looking into the rearview mirror, she sees
pictures her daughter, probably grown by now,
had drawn on the steaming glass of the back window —
a lopsided heart, a cat without a tail. The headlights
of the only other car on the road make glittering eyes
in the cat's round stomach. The road is littered
with corpses, raccoon, opossum, skunk,
their glittering entrails livid on the moonstruck asphalt.
She thinks of the crows, the next morning,
waiting for a break in the traffic.

The Pyromaniac and the Heat Wave

At last it comes, stealing
into her room at night,
pulling back the sheet
and nudging her gown above her thighs.
She sighs at the familiar
touch and longs for morning
when it will funnel its full force
through the round eye she has always
loved. Outside, the moonstruck
shadows of palm applaud the hot wind.

As a child she feared the dark
dreams and waited in her bed
for the sun's certain climb, for her mother
to move softly through the room
shutting off the blazing lamps,
knowing now her child could sleep.

So tonight she will prepare herself,
paint her lips and brush her hair
electric, thinking already
of the day rearranged,
the night sky lit with a million filaments,
how then she can sing herself to sleep
in a child's breathy voice,
"Fire, fire, fire, fire,
the hills are burning, the hills are burning."

Mother, Retelling the News

For weeks you follow the case
of the doctor who must have hated
his wife. The evidence points
against him — a saw blade with its telling
film, his boat moored on the Mississippi.
They release him because her head remains
a missing technicality. You call
your youngest daughter, married
for thirteen years to a surgeon
and oblivious in California, to tell her the news.
At that very moment her husband's gloved hand
enters an open chest and holds the willing heart.

Tonight you sew in your finished basement
bent over yards of enshrouding silk
aligning the stitches like words.
It is dark except for the intense light
on your hands I want to believe in.
You tell me another story, the false one
about what happens when someone steps on a needle,
the fine steel heading straight for the calling heart.

My Student, Talking

After the classroom routine
you come to my office where books tilt
dangerously on the shelves above our heads
and the sun through the blinds
paints our faces crazy. You know all
your poems by heart. The first is something
about a high window, one foot
on the sill. *The next time
I let them take me. Listen!*

I push off and my chair slides
across the carpet on silent wheels.
Our knees nearly touch. You inch away,
heels stuttering like a shot cowboy's,
but you're already up against the wall.
*Listen! Blade and rope, the seductive
pill, black water rising.* For the next
one you stand, saying you need
more air. I tell you I know
what you mean. *Listen! Someone's
inside me.* You pull your beard
and it comes off in your hand.
You open your shirt
and your chest is transparent
as the anatomical man's
in grade school science class.
Listen! I'm in a cage.
You open it and your heart
flies out. Finally it falls
at my feet. Listen.

Under Glass

Santa Maria della Vittoria

The church is a window to another
world that asks me to shut out the rest
of Rome and step into the fifteenth century
stories in marble and stone
telling of the thorns, the bones,
offering proof — the heart, the left
shoe — to make faith a fact,
to urge the arresting photograph.

So here lies the body under glass, a saint,
her gown embellished with its blinding stars,
her head arranged on two embroidered cushions
that bend her neck to breaking. This
to display the martyring
wound, her slit throat
issuing painted droplets just renewed.
She is no longer amused by the predictable.
Knowing this, it occurs to me
to stylize every gesture,
enunciate every syllable, just in case,
in the split second all heads are diverted,
one eye opens
and invites me deeper than I ever dreamed.

Questions

Oh I talk long distance at midnight
and say how I miss you
but postpone my return
and dream about an old lover
I haven't seen for months.

Then breakfast with an Italian Jew
driven from Europe by the Germans
and she understands their language
but never speaks it anymore.
She says the hand-laid parquet floor
in her dining room was worth ten grand
but she wouldn't sell and then
when the house went she got nothing
and what does my husband do?
I say I'm divorcing him
and she shrugs.

But later his lawyer wants to know
why I left and asks about my sex life.
I think he might be German.
I forget the questions or I answer in Italian.

Liar

I know a man born with no
conception, no one
to charge with neglect.
His first words enlarged
the language of lies.
He squatted and rocked on his heels
practicing his *hiss*. And now
some mornings when he wakes after rain,
the sky is too vacant to remember anything.
The lies have settled
at the back of his brain,
against the rising years.
At night, snoring fitfully toward
the heaven of liars, he dreams,
in his unrest, of the first covering,
a rustle of leaves over the place
where the first woman lay.

Waiting for This

One day in November the subway will rattle into the station,
pick up a passenger waiting in rough weather,
and carry her to the divorce lawyer
composed in the glass cage of his office
high above the coiling river.
He will take her hand in both of his, her fingers
fluttering against his palms. Help, they say.
We cannot see. We are afraid of the dark
tunnel of your imagination.

The windows are walls,
the room alive with light.
She will squint in the glare, unable to see
past the thick blank lenses that correct his sight.
His bald head gleams like another eye.
She will not listen to the clatter of words
spilling like perpetual derailment from his thick lips,
but hear instead the last leaves
on the November trees scraping each other.

He snaps the long cord to shut the blinds
and cuts out the sky with a clatter.
Then he will hover above her,
tilt his shining head so it looks
half severed, and force his tongue into her mouth.
She has a scar that arcs from hip bone to hip bone,
the tired history of her body.

She will smoke while she waits for the subway home.
The platform is deserted on that November night,
but her pockets bulge with ritual pills,
desperate lists:

> Read no paragraph more than twice
> Postpone all illness
> Never marry a man who will hate you
> Hold your life in your own hands

The train will shriek into the tunnel
ripping her with the round eye of its light.
The leaves are down all over.

Dream at Easter

I leave the meat
in the alley
with the dogs,
lay it tenderly
on the cracked brick
as though it were an altar
and I some supplicant.
It is pungent,
warm with spice.
After three days,
still no mark
of tooth or careless claw.
The dogs continue circling.

Aquarium

First they are color,
words for blue:
inkblot,
blueprint,
held breath,
innocent eyes,
blood in the vein,
lapis lazuli,
new bruise,
madder blue,
charged peacock,
pills beside the bed,

or words for green:
bottle glass,
boa,
camouflage,
elusive wing,
apprenticeship,
cellar stair,
lost key,
a price to pay,
highest roof in Rome,
sick of everything.

Then they are names:
damsel, clown,
coral toadfish hairy chin,
flameback angel burning wing,
holy mackerel, crimson rover,
midnight parrot eager beak,
reef shark, hammerhead,
sapphire eel bites for keeps.

They linger in the eyes,
surface on the tongue.
Fish in the brain,
fish in the blood,
a hook in the heart
pulling tight.

Anger

For you the variegated plain
is one color,
the sunrise a smear
on the horizon,
the blackbird no more
than its red wing.

Now, on the telephone in anger,
your voice a tension,
the highest wire.
This is hate, a deadly sin,
for which I have no retort,
and the telephone lines
will not blow down.
At least don't count on it.
So I retreat,
hold the receiver away from my ear.
Disappear mid-syllable,
old ghost, I say,
and push the magic button.

But still
I have a picture of you,
a hair-raising sequel to yourself,
rattling the ice in your Scotch
like anger you cannot dissolve.

What She Knows

Waking, she still knows
the answer. The perfect words
show themselves like the pure notes
the pianist on his deathbed
sees as light held
in the undeserving air.

Gratefully she makes her way
through the dark
house. At her desk, the high intensity
lamp cuts its sudden circle
on the blank page. She writes the words
in a language she doesn't know
she knows. There is no

happiness like hers. Then sleep
announces itself as a dark figure
who pushes his fingers into her eyes.
She, with her weakness for the dark,
cannot refuse. She goes back to bed
believing the words
will live on the warm page
and dreams there is life inside her.
The doctor delivers a thumb-sized baby
with a silver spoon.

The next morning, in the quiet house,
she knows the infant
has not survived the night.

The Sickness of the Body

Alley lady crazy in scarves,
dead now,
prowled with her cats at night
and scared children.
I was five when I nursed six black kittens
sick on their rags
then picked sores on my arms
at their grave.

One night in a dream
I shot ponies
for food.
It was a good idea.
Then, strung out on snow,
the dilemma of carcasses,
the red on my hands.

I could take my body
to Montego Bay
and sit poor on porch steps
smoking ganja,
talking in thick air
about old sorrow.

Dreaming of the Dead

1

I recognize most of them. There is the man
with watery eyes who says he loves
me too much, even now, to stop looking
back. And grandmother, who is tired
this visit, shuffles down the long hall
in her run-over slippers, her small dog
nipping at her hands. "Nothing is ever
final," she says with a German accent,
and stoops to pet the dog. She's looking
for her son again, even though he's standing
behind her. She can't see the neat hole
above his right ear. When he whispers
he's slept long enough, the dog snarls
realistically.

2

This time your funeral's in a cathedral
with a maze ending at the coffin,
but we don't have to walk on our knees.
Some children, in fact, are running
with roses streaming from their hair.
Seconds before I turn the last
corner, you settle comfortably
in your glass aquarium case. I imagine
your eyes behind your Blues Brothers glasses.
If I had married you, I'd almost be a widow.

3

When I'm awake, they think I don't notice
their restless gestures: the altered
angle of the bureau mirror tilted
to reflect the white ceiling; the missing
pages from Rachmaninoff's *Prelude*,
the ones my hands didn't memorize; or
the bird reciting words I didn't teach him
then staring at some point beyond me
when I ask *how,* and *who.*

But now, because I'm asleep,
Mr. Watery Eyes inches up from the foot
of the bed reaching as he did in life,
the electrocuted prom queen brushes her hair
in front of the bureau mirror
stroking herself into static, a woman I don't know
tries on my blue flowered dress and finds it
a perfect fit but not to her liking.
The small dog races through them
barking himself insane. More are knocking
on the door. "Come in," I say, opening
my arms. "Touch me again. Deeper."

Bending to Look Through Your Eyes

Musée Marmottan

Your glasses in the museum case
tell why you gave up looking
for the whole story. The mismatched
lenses, one convex the other flat,
detail the last half-blind years
when boats sailed over the horizon
and spires rose as believers prayed they would.

One afternoon in the sunstruck garden,
you turn to the trembling hyacinth
and wait for the rioting blooms to assume
a formal pose. At last, you think,
the world is small enough. Then, tracing
the thin wires rimming the perimeters of sight,
you tell someone who barely knows you, "It's not
the nightmare you might think, you who find
another's tragedy more tragic than your own."

And now, bending to look through your eyes,
I see you pause beneath a single branch.
But when you raise your head, the wavering
blossoms cloud the glass for one brief moment
before form and color fuse,
before the world shuts down.

A Plan to Circumvent the Death of Beauty

Because she thinks it can be bought, she fills
her windows with hibiscus in glamorous pots
to hide the fact of high-rise brick.
Some nights she wants to float the magenta blossoms
in shallow dishes on the piano lid,
tie a red-fringed shawl around her waist
and play mazurkas by heart while dreaming of dancing.
But after one season, the perfect blooms are spent
and now, stunted, rootbound, the stems rot from the inside out.

Then she remembers the rows of pet store aquariums,
the stunning neon fish grazing above miniature divers.
(This is almost the same story.) Only one of them lives, a black
angel with tattered wings treading the algae-dark water.
In her dreams it grows enormous, amorous, more
dangerous than flesh. As a child, her least favorite
uncle, a farmer, watched her swing on the gate to the sty.
He said, "A sow like that'll take a man's leg off."

Enticed by the pale filaments of its expressive crest,
seduced by the enviable dark pools of its eyes that see out
both sides at once, its sexual tongue, she buys
a cockatoo in an elegant wrought iron cage.
When she dreams she can fly beyond the steep faces
of the brick buildings, the exhausting air,
the corridors of winter trees, she looks down
and sees her mother, only thirty,
framed by the doorway of the family home,
the trellises alive with blooms. Her mother
is beautiful, black hair fanned by the breeze.
Shading her eyes, she tilts back her head
and crows at the flying girl who drops
her arms, all the light dissolving around her.

Going Under

Sierra Vista Hospital

The needle convinces me
to quit without a struggle.
In truth, there is little
I want to keep: the last time
with my lover, my daughter's honest eyes,
a moment of private glory. These
I hold like a few flowers
in a competent hand.

Then fingers loosen round the stems,
red and yellow blossoms drift
from the neat frame of vision. It is
so easy. Not nearly as arduous
as coming back to the full field
with neither choice nor right.

III

Refugees At Avila Beach

Every day sandpipers track their reflections across the sand,
their slick elusive perfect selves,
then run from the waves they pursued.
I lean heavily on my sister's arm, too sick
to follow the water. I see myself,
two bent miniatures, one in each of her pupils.

We cross the road to a seaside inn
run at little profit by an old Mexican and his brassy wife.
They tell us about the Filipino who comes once a week
for chili before his fishing trip: "Those Filipinos
use every part of their catch." I saw him myself,
hunched on a stool, looking poor.

Restless, I have traveled across seven states
to say nothing. She is sister, yes,
split from the same home, but thirty years
of free passage have dropped her on this distant coast
she cannot leave. I shade my eyes and turn to the window
where I can still see the sandpipers: one flaps
off to the left in neat evasion.

We walk back up the coast to the car.
The fisherman hauls in his nets, a meager catch.
The sun drags its slow flame toward
the horizon. All night long the birds
will sleep on the Pacific, rocking uneasily.

Regarding Marie Antoinette

I start near the end
of the story, circling the Place de la Concorde
all afternoon looking for the exact
spot where you lost your head.
Someone said the guillotine
stood at the statue of Brest, but
there is no clue, no perceptible red. Instead,
a high fashion model, blue lips
and yellow hair, poses for the photographer.
Then touring the Law Courts, there is no time
to view your cell, and somehow
I overlook the display at the Musée Grévin
where a wax figure wearing your clothes
stands by the transposed prison door
at which you must have knocked
or wept. Finally I stop
at the royal necropolis. It is impossible
to tell which unmarked slab holds you in place.

But still I know how you waited
out the Paris summer,
scanning the same sky I see now
alone on the midnight balcony.
Birds beat the air
with a sound like tumbrels
as they circle the lighted towers,
and the thin-bladed moon
poses its single truth.
There is hardly time to regard
the rooftops time has rearranged
before relenting to the tireless sky
and admitting at last
this kingdom was never mine.

Edens Expressway: An Ode

An unfinished stretch
shows how it's done: graded
dirt, sand, gravel, mesh,
concrete, a difficult stratum.

Barebacked men
in their important squads
take time to huddle with their rakes
and tell of nights with women.

At their call, the heaviest
equipment comes — the gravel truck,
cement truck, water truck,
all night in caravans, their headlights
distant pairs of moons.
They build the road for months,
each man keeping pace
until the rhythm's public.

It's a new geology,
sublime enough to take a driver
to the rim of the moving moon.

Shortcut Through the Park

We have started out as we should
on the slick sidewalks,
our useless umbrella catching the wind.
We have a destination in this downpour
and it is too late to turn back.

The park is paved with worms.
Gaslamps line the path
spotlighting their long bodies,
palpable and shining,
convulsing so deliberately
I can no longer tell myself
they are harmless, blind,
or lost and longing for their dark home.
I tell you they're all around us,
risen sins familiar as my own mind's dark.
Each contraction and expansion
spells out a knowledge of what
lies beneath the surface.

There is no place to step with certainty,
but your thick-soled boots
never break stride.
Breathless, I bob at your shoulder,
every step a dodge.

Venus de Milo: Her Final Complaint

It's not me they adore,
the critics and comedians,
the know-nothing scholars
with their bags of spare parts
and flawed imaginations.
I could tell them I never held
an apple or rested against a pillar
as they say. If we were speaking,
Victory would advise, "You
know who you are," but she still
finds every flashbulb a thrill.

Or I could tell them Victory folds
her wings at night, she who is first
admired, reigning, as she does
over the center hall and great stair.
No one ever needs to ask, "Where's Victory?"
No one could entice her to desert her ship

but she would be tempted
by the vision of miraculous ascent,
she would be prompted by the image
of dumbfounded tourists fumbling
with their cameras, too rapt to believe
anything except they have captured
the true cross or robe. But for me
the question was never glory,

and so it will come to this: the first
unsteady step from my small pedestal,
the warm goodbyes to the others
in my crowded hall who wish me well,
who press me to accept what I need —
a left foot, two arms with hands,
the true history of twenty centuries.
Victory, asleep on the landing,
will not awake when I break the glass
of the nearby case to take the palm
and ring finger credited to her.
Capable, complete, I will descend,
my reliable feet silent on the marble stair,
my robe billowing behind me like wings.

Dreamer, 3:00 A.M.

Sleep spreads out before her like a pond,
bottomless and warm, dark
with muck thrashed up by snake and fish.

Her legs fuse into a capable fin,
her waist grows thin, her lungs
unlearn the air. Now
an easy arch of her back
carries her the full length of the pond.
In such a world, a flash of fin
or a slight shift in the wind
tells a whole story.

But sleep will not let her forget
her waking world, her mortal self
who walks to the edge of the pond and asks,
even in the middle of the dive,
even as the hard fact of the water
rushes up to meet her,
to soar forever.

Two Mallards

They move where they choose, I think,
in the uneasy lake. The surface
should be simpler. I'm safe
against your body on the bank.
Women in their summer shoes
totter among lilacs in the park behind us.
We don't speak to anyone.

Later, alone in the city where I was born,
hundreds of miles between us,
two mallards in father's creek
come to eat corn shelled by hand.
They totter up the hill on their webbed feet
like sick children. The male stretches
his green neck. I bribe them closer, but think
back to the water...going is easier there.

If I strayed down by the footbridge,
could I feel you again beside me?
You touch, sly as a feather.

Tropics

The view from the veranda
is explicit. The overwhelming green
of the breadfruit tree repeats
its single image: two bold orbs
flanking a fleshy bud.
A lizard on the nearest branch
pulses its yellow pouch,
exhales its slender tongue.

Wild hibiscus open themselves
in a red profusion, and coconut palms
flaunt their bright globes
inviting the imagination into their milky
interiors. The full lips
of the ackee enfold their round black
centers. Everywhere, the unpurchasable
opulence.

Even so early the air is palpable,
outlining the body like a damp sheet.
The lizard pumps up and down on its
forelegs. I glimpse you through the overgrowth
walking up the dirt road toward the house.
Closer, I see the sweat on your forehead,
the spreading stain.

Ground Blizzard

You are in this alone.
When your ticking heart
lost under layers
of heavy clothes
no longer consoles you,
the steering wheel's
obliging grooves
ask you to believe
it's a hand you hold.

But if you could rise
above the flying snow
you would find
the cloud line wavering
like the shadows
of blue mountains,
and when it tempts
you past that dark mass
holding you close
to what you know,
the open sky exhales
its breathable air
unmasking a country
the color of a flamingo
whose wing shapes
whatever story you want.
Then you forget forever
the two red taillights
you've been made to follow
your whole life, the eyes
burning in a face
you cannot see.

How the Twentieth Century Betrayed the Last Christian Martyr

This is a story
about a German tourist who lost
his mind in the basilica
at St. Gatien. Although I was
there, I cannot explain
everything. But I have seen
St. Denis carrying his head
across the murals and stained
glass, and of course I have heard
about Sebastian, Agnes, and Joan.

Now here they stand,
a three star line-up
at the basilica's portals.
Such symmetry of broken bones
and more than a little dirty!
What witch hunt could find
the missing noses, the toes?

Our tourist — I'll call him Gustof
after a distant relative maimed
in war — admires the gargoyles
leaning toward him, working
their shocked mouths. But he
answers, "Vive la France!" too loud
to be talking to anyone.
Stopping to read the capitals'
crumbling stories, he sees
Eve's eager reach and Adam
tremble, Cain's bowstring quiver
and Abel recline against a tree.

Inside, the basilica's eternal
space calls to him
like a painted child
rising from the mouth of the good
thief. Gustof, too, wants
to loosen his grip and drift
toward the unthinkable height,
then drop his life like a white egg
he's always sheltered.

When his friend sets up a tripod
to capture the rose window, Gustof
sees the built fire ignite.
Drawing his umbrella to defend
the church, he jousts the length
of the nave. The mad
blows pierce the unblinking saints
and stun the speechless friend
whose struck fingers
loll like cut tongues.

When the gendarmes haul him
outside, past the scaffold
and tumbling spires,
his heart beats faster
but no one will cut it out.

Looking for You One Year Later

To my sister

The fog doles everything out.
First the cattle drowsy on the mountain's flank,
higher up the houses of the rich
unwavering on their stilts,
and by noon the jagged peak
aligned with the sun.
Every morning Mount Madonna heaves into shape
pulling its cargo into plain view.

One year ago our talk
wound like bougainvillea in the arbor —
too many blooms to count.
Your hands darted
for emphasis, brilliant as hummingbirds
in the yard's border of Nile queen.

But now you are rich and your husband
has had his first affair. You float
on a raft in the sapphire center
of your swimming pool
trailing one jeweled hand in the water.
I try to think of you as uninjured.
If we could talk, I would tell you
what I know of pain: the burn on my hand
has healed. The scar fades daily.
I stay on the chaise,
pretending to read.

Each morning of this visit
I wait for the view to complete itself,
for the winds of San Luis
to blow the shroud from the peak
and reveal things
as they were.

Harbor Seal

He is not dead or even visibly injured,
but he's out of the water and doesn't scare
when our group of hikers troops along
the breakwater rimming his patch of beach.
The leader points him out: "Look, a harbor seal."
We obediently train our binoculars
on his sleek body, examining him inch by inch
like a lost child come home. For his part,
he leans over backward to see us, nose pointed up
but without a striped ball to balance.

Settling down among the rocks with our lunches,
we toss crumbs at the blue crabs
and wave to the pelicans collapsing into the Pacific.
From time to time we draw the seal into focus
to check for change. When there is none,
one of us, a man, climbs down the rocks to the beach,
picking up a piece of driftwood on his way.
He follows an imaginary path of ever
smaller concentric circles which trap
the seal at their center. Then, only a few feet away,
the man hunches over and holds the driftwood
in front of him like a long arm, a pose
he remembers from television or some deeper past.
The seal, his neck a swivel, follows the man with his eyes
but does not advance or retreat. Finally

I go home to the warm house where my children
cheer my return. I empty my pockets
and give them sand dollars the size of quarters,
dark feathers and mussel shells. I tell them
how a sea hare big as a foot shot its dye
into the shallows, staining the water, the sand,
how the color oozed between my fingers,
how it stained my hands the purest purple.

7:00 A.M. Lakefront

When the wind roars in from the east like this,
the lake is all spray shot up
like island palms splayed against the sky.
At each rock the surface bursts
then heals itself against the shore.

Back in the grass
wrens sputter themselves clean in a pool of sand,
on the beach a passionate couple grapples
on a paisley blanket, and waddling gulls
fling themselves up in a single motion
netting the sky with their wings.

Out there no land is in sight, no safe harbor
in the heave and spasm vacant as sea.
From where I stand the sun-glazed waves
look solid enough to walk on. So it may
have seemed to you in April, 1932,
when you stepped from the deck of the *Orizaba*,
giving up your body to the sea.

Strasbourg in the Spring: A Guided Walk

Trust me when I tell you
to begin at the river Lill,
to walk the corridor of weeping
willows and dazzling chestnuts
with blooms erect as Christmas candles.
Follow its insinuations
toward the wooden footbridge and locks
announcing the old city.
Stop on the bridge and look back
to marvel how river, trees, and path
converge where you stand.

Now you are ready to turn
toward the row of half-timbered houses
built right on the edge.
There you admire the window box pinks and blues
naive as weather and finally choose
the second house, the one with a brass
knocker shaped like the angel
of death. Touch her wing, her rib
if you must, but do not try to tip
the hourglass. Because no one answers,
you believe the house empty. Stepping inside,
you taste the warm loaf
cooling on the table. You are drawn
to the daguerreotype above the mantel.
Note how the face resembles yours.

Looking outside, you discover the sinking
sun has changed everything. When you decide
to let it go, turn into the dim hall.
You find your way to the back
bedroom and sit on the white coverlet.
Think of yourself as young,
a girl waving from a high window.
Now you notice a woman in a black
veil lying beside you. Ask her
if she remembers growing old.
When she does not answer,
tell her you have spent your life
searching for her. Then clasp
her hand, a perfect fit, and finally
admit you understand. Believe me
when I tell you I want nothing more.

Waking in Another Country

for Nancy Cook

We board the train as we must
and without direction from us,
it begins its competent climb.
Rocking in our berths, put away
for the night, the countries slip
by. You do not wake me at the tunnel
where terrorists once left the passengers
dead, but now at the 2:00 A.M. border
you rouse me from a dream
of safe sunshine and blazing poppies
saying, "See how the architecture
has changed, how chateau becomes
chalet." The window gives back
nothing but my own face
backlit against the Alps, the high-speed
stationary view I have always expected.

Riding the Back Bay Trail

The horses are willing
but do not know the way.
As for me, I am always lost.
Sister, everything depends
on you: the whole weight
of the great animals,
their expansive flanks
and fears. You guide

us into the shifting dunes
where every step is labor.
The mounds surround us
like the bodies of enormous women
reclined, and we become
smaller than life: you on Desperado,
a black spot against the pale sand,
and me on Sheba, old paint,
following like a faithful dog.
Always it is climb and descent.
Foam flashes from the horses' mouths.

When we consider turning back,
the Pacific surges across the horizon.
We glimpse it at each rise
until, as in a childhood dream
fulfilled, we move like centaurs
onto the level beach. Caught up
by the cool air, I urge
Sheba toward the waves
you say will hypnotize her,
draw her in. I don't tell you
how well I understand
or that I recognize this
as the best end.
When she refuses, I still
understand. Turning her away,

you talk to me of loss —
of your husband who has left you
again. We plod up and down the beach
until the shore birds expect us
and the single fisherman
doesn't turn his head.

You choose a different trail
for the return, to confuse the horses
so they won't run home.
In the eucalyptus grove
among identical trunks
and forking paths, again
we pass the lost shoe,
the broken lantern,
proving we have memorized
landmarks to nowhere.
The woman watching
from the hillside house
believes our choices are obvious
as the lines in her face.

Suddenly the horses' ears pitch
forward, as if hearing their stablemates
whinneying them home.
Then we see the barn
high in the darkening hills.
Leaving the trail,
we forge through scrub
and chaparral, the thorny branches
biting at our boots.
I think of Sheba's vulnerable body,
I hear her heavy breath,
the exhalations of complaint,
the lost faith.

Jade Cove

An old woman scuttles down
the embankment, her eyes already
fixed on the stones. She carries
a net bag and a forked stick.
Her rubber boots slap against her calves.
She plans how she will begin
by the patch of seaweed and kelp
blazing with flies and work her way toward
a fortune. She will stay close
to the water to claim what the waves
throw at her feet. She thinks her surprise
will be like the fisherman's who hoists
his net from the dark sea and is blinded
by the one golden fish leaping
and leaping, moving his mouth.

Now the woman stands with her back
to the water and imagines her fish
caught in the pool of light
dying behind the hills. The waves pull
at her ankles, wresting the jade
right out from under her,
but she does not know of her loss.
The last sunbathers swathed in towels
struggle up the embankment. The waves
heave themselves higher, as if to swallow
the woman who still believes
she can will the fish into her net.

Printing by Crouse Printing, Champaign, Illinois
Cover Illustration by Darryl Johnson
Back Cover Photograph by Roy Lundelius